This book has been dedicated to the worlds dyslexics.

Four Williams and Me!

Volume 1

First edition
2004

To Lesley

with Lots of Love

Bryan
xxx

Published by
Dyslexic Publications UK

Introduction

Dyslexia is a lifetime medical condition that brings with it a host of problems such as reading prescriptions, mail, contracts, food labels, subtitles, menus in restaurants and so on. Living with dyslexia can bring on depression, anxiety and stress. These are very serious and very real problems.

Four Williams and Me! Has been designed not only to help dyslexics with their reading and writing but also to help non-dyslexics to understand some of the difficulties dyslexics have to live with every day.

If there was only one or two dyslexics then you could understand the complacency often shown by non-dyslexics. Given that there is an estimated four and a half million of us living in the UK alone, then you have to ask the question - why?

It is easy to walk past a person in a wheelchair and notice they have a disability but ask yourself this, if that person had fallen out, would you have helped them? I think it is fair to say that you would. As the pace of life gets faster I have found it more and more difficult to do the simplest of things, i.e. going shopping is easy to a non-dyslexic but when I ask for assistance I am often told to go and find the item I require myself.

If they removed all the words on all the products in the supermarket I wonder how a non-dyslexic would manage?!

Once I have found a product I like, I tend to stay with it only because I recognise the colour or the shape. This works well for me until the company decides to change the look of their products.

Dyslexia is a real problem for a large number of people; the statistics show that all non-dyslexics know at least one. Find out who it is in your circle and see how you can help them.

Sir Winston Churchill got help from his friends and look how he repaid them!

A few facts about Dyslexia

Sir Winston Churchill, William Blake, Richard Branson, Susan Hampshire and Anthea Turner all suffer, or suffered, with dyslexia.

Up to 70% of inmates in British prisons are dyslexic.

97% of employers insist on written qualifications.

It has been estimated that there are more adult dyslexics in the United Kingdom than the combined populations of Malta, Luxembourg, Iceland, Bahrain, Kuwait, Barbados, Grenada, St. Lucia and Belize!

Dyslexia is hereditary and affects a higher percentage of boys than girls.

Four Williams and me! works in part by picture association. The first known people to use this system were the ancient Egyptians over 4000 years ago.

Arial is widely recognised as the best font for dyslexics.

Sadly there is no cure for dyslexia.

The Non-Dyslexic

How does this book help dyslexics?

The diagram opposite shows the parts of the brain that processes information. Images are recorded onto the pad and written text onto the loop. You will notice in particular that in the loop all the disks are shaded, indicating that it is working perfectly - a non-dyslexic.

It is this loop that causes dyslexics to run into problems from a very young age. Beneath the loop is a narrow channel, allowing enough room for the information stored on the loop to pass from the short-term memory into the long-term memory.

There are 11 disks in both the non-dyslexic and the dyslexics brain however, the difference appears when some of these disks fail to function. Only three of my disks work making me an average dyslexic.

Okay, but what do you mean?

We all learn how to spell and read in virtually the same way. This is by our infant school teacher writing words on a board in front of the class and asking us to copy them, this method is perfect for non-dyslexics but not for dyslexics.

An example please!

The teacher writes the word DOG on the board, I then write this in my textbook but at the same time I am putting each letter from the word onto the loop in my brain.

I have room for all the letters so they instantly pass down to my long-term memory - perfect - I will never forget how to spell DOG.

When the teacher writes a longer word like INSURANCE for instance, I am in trouble. A non-dyslexic will put all nine letters onto their loop and pass it straight down into the long-term memory. I however, can only cope with INS then URA and then NCE, so my long-term memory will save this combination. Therefore, when I need to spell insurance I will struggle.

If you repeat this method with every word I have learnt and then multiply it by the years I spent at school, the result you will see is me. Just one of many adults with the literary skills of a very young child or, to put it another way, a dyslexic.

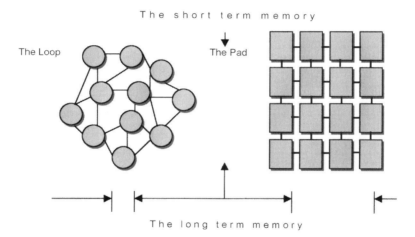

The short term memory

The Loop

The Pad

The long term memory

Fig A: The Non-Dyslexic

The Dyslexic

The most important thing to remember is that you are not alone. There are an estimated 4,500,000 adult dyslexics in the UK, 18,000,000 in the U.S.A and 1,000,000 in Australia.

To understand how the dyslexics brain works, the diagram opposite will help to explain. There are four parts to remember.

The loop shown on the top left, the pad shown on the top right, the short-term memory is shown as the smaller top section and the long-term memory is shown as the larger section at the bottom.

The Loop

The loop takes letters from words and places one letter into each of the 11 disks i.e. the word CAT contains three letters and would be split up by the loop and stored as C.A.T. This is then sent from the short-term memory to the long-term memory for future use.

The Pad

The pad stores images and places them on each of the 16 disks. i.e. if you were to look at a car, a bike and a boat each of these items would be stored onto three individual disks and then sent from the short-term memory to the long-term memory for future use.

The Short-term Memory

The short-term memory can only hold on to information for a short time. The loop and the pad need to be clear to make way for more information. The cleared information is passed into the long-term memory for storage. The channel beneath the loop is smaller than the one beneath the pad making the pad a more efficient source for processing information.

The Long-term Memory

The long-term memory is why we can function on a day to day basis, without this we would simply not exist. Everything we do, say and think comes from the long-term memory. It is like the hard drive of a computer only considerably more powerful. Everything that goes into the long-term memory stays there forever.

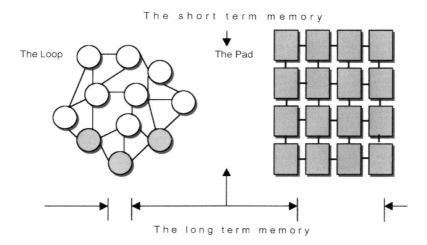

Fig B: The Dyslexic

Strengths and Weaknesses

To understand this book fully, it is important to test yourself. Here is a simple way to do it.

All you need to do is write down as many words as you can on a single sheet of paper and then ask a non-dyslexic to spell check them.

For example:

If you have listed 100 words and 10 are spelt correctly, simply take the average number of letters from the longest to the shortest words. This number will give you an approximate idea as to the number of disks you have working in your loop. If you find that all the words you have written are correct, then I hope you enjoy the images.

If you score around 5, then work through this book looking up any words you are unfamiliar with, and once you have got to the stage where you can recite from just seeing the corresponding picture to the text, then do the test again. If your score increases then you are on the first rung of the ladder. Practice will make perfect.

Is there anything I could do to improve my spelling?

You can improve your spelling by changing letters into everyday images. For example, I walk through the Atrium past the Bowling centre to the Car park - ABC. Carry this through the whole alphabet and by becoming very familiar with this journey, you will be able to look at any word and instead of seeing letters, you will see your images. These images relate to parts of your journey and by placing this information onto the pad, you will be able to store the information into your long-term memory for future use.

At the back of the book you will find five images without text, this has been done deliberately to allow you to freely express yourself in your own unique way.

Alternatively, you can find other works by Shakespeare, Hazlitt, Words-worth and Blake and add them to the images.

She was a phantom of delight,
when first she gleamed
upon my sight.

Love is too young to
know what conscience is

William Shakespeare

Family bonds (Australia)

Best friends (Australia)

There is a smile of love
and there is a smile of deceit,
and there is a smile of smiles
in which these two smiles meet.

William Blake

Born of nothing
Begot of nothing

William Hazlitt

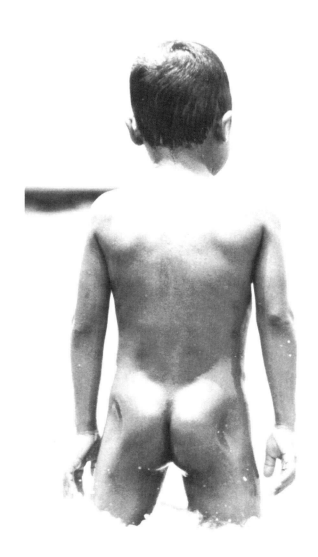

Marday (Bali)

Holding on (Italy)

Love seeketh
not itself to please,
nor for itself half any care
but for another
gives its ease
and builds a heaven
in hells despair.

William Blake

One might believe
that natural miseries
had blasted France,
and made of it a land
unfit for men,

William Wordsworth

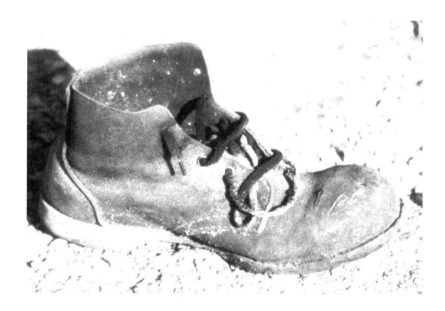

Wars end (France)

Winter light (UK)

The seasons came,
and my notice brought
a store of transitory qualities

Tis not my present purpose
to retrace that variegated
journey step by step:

William Wordsworth

River crossing (Australia)

Mountain air (Australia)

I see two consciousnesses,
conscious of myself
and of some other being,
a grey stone of native rock

William Wordsworth

A sense of power and
sublimity coming
over the mind

William Hazlitt

Water's edge (Australia)

Captain Cook's Endeavour (World's Oceans)

This ship
was nought to me,
nor I to her,
yet I pursued her
with a lover's look;
this ship to all the rest
did I prefer.

William Wordsworth

And now I see
with eyes serene
the very pulse
of the machine

William Wordsworth

Saluting the day (World's Oceans)

Houses of Parliament (London)

I wander thr'o
each chartered street,
near where the
chartered Thames
does flow,
and mark in
every face I meet
marks of weakness,
marks of woe

William Blake

When looking on the
present face of things,
I see one man, of men
the meanest too!
raised up to sway
the world, to do
undo,
with mighty nations,

Preparation (USA)

Stakeout (Croatia)

It is sordid,
Servile,
Inert,
a compound of
Dullness'
Vanity
and interest

William Haslitt

To be, or not to be:
that is the question:
whether tis nobler in
the mind to suffer
the, slings and arrows
of outrageous fortune,
or to take arms against
a sea of troubles,
and by opposing end them?

Sculptured form (Germany)

Thirst (Great Sandy Desert)

I only look for
pain and grief
and trembled as
I drew more near;
but God`s unbounded
love is here,
and I have found relief

William Wordsworth

That which is true
or beautiful in itself,
is not the less so
for standing alone

William Haslitt

Balance (Moscow)

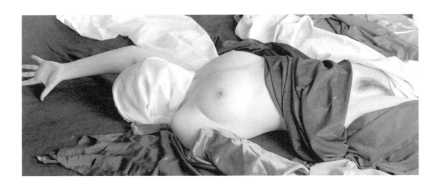

The eagerness of
infantine desire?
a tranquillizing spirit
presses now
on my corporeal frame

William Wordsworth

In the age of gold,
free from winter's cold,
youth and maiden
bright to the holy light,
naked
in the sunny beams delight

William Blake

Shadows (Holland)

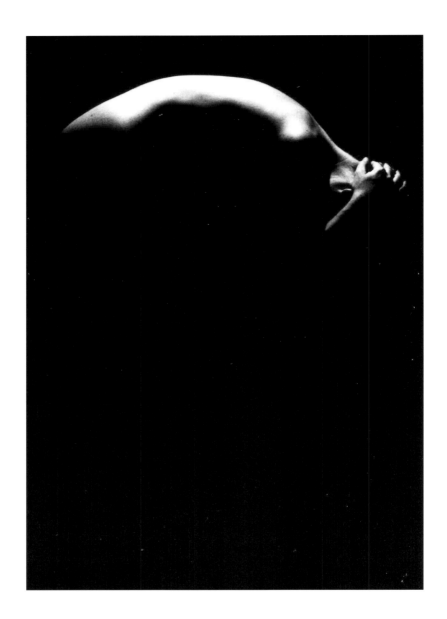

Back lit (Moscow)

Beauty truth and rarity
grace in all simplicity

William Shakespeare

I will build
thee a labyrinth
(where we may
remain forever alone)

William Blake

Morning mist (Java)

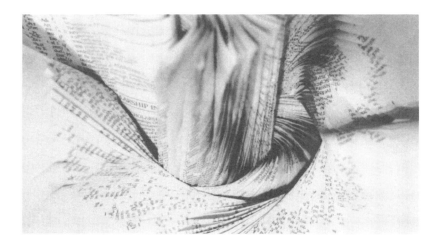

The written word (Canada)

I dreamt a dream!
what can it mean?
and that I was a
maiden queen,
guarded by an
angel mild,
witless woe was
ne`er beguil`d!

William Blake

Dark revolving in silent activity
unseen in tormenting passions

William Blake

London Eye (UK)

Ice (New York City)

If music be the food of love
Play on

William Shakespeare

His little nameless,
unremembered
acts of kindness
and of love

William Shakespeare

Ciba (Queensland)

Danni (Australia)

Beauty itself doth of itself
persuade the eye of man
without an orator

William Shakespeare

I follow him to
serve my turn
upon him

William Blake

Bandana (Caribbean)

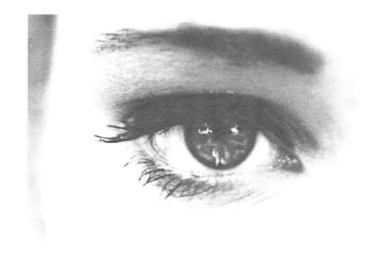

Lipstick (Milan)

Thou blind fool,
love,
what dost thou to
mine eyes,
that behold,
and see not
what they see?

Love looks not with the eyes,
but with the mind;
and therefore is winged
cupid painted blind

William Shakespeare

Jo (Amsterdam)

The hidden Buddha (Java)

Let me
look back upon thee

William Shakespeare

Pity would be no
more if we did not
make somebody poor;
and mercy no more
could be, if all were as
happy as we

William Blake

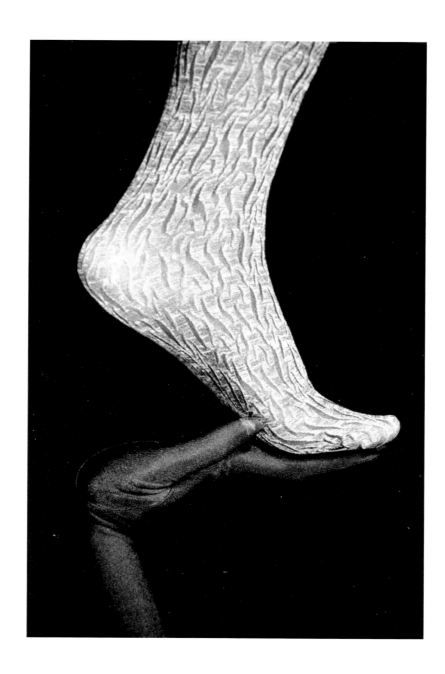

A helping hand (Spain)

Close fit (Mexico City)

Cruelty has a
human heart,
and jealousy a
human face;
terror the human
form divine,
and secrecy the
human dress.

William Blake

To look like nobody else
is a sufficiently
mortifying reflection

William Hazlitt

Hands upon my heart (UK)

Nought loves another as itself,
nor venerates another so,
nor is it possible to thought
a greater than itself to know

William Blake

Love and joy or twins

William Hazlitt

Ripening fruit (Morocco)

Touch (Thailand)

These two are
such as one,
that they may be
distinguished
indeed in thought,
but not in act

William Blake

But now upon the
written leaf I
look indeed with
pain and grief

William Wordsworth

Rainforest (Borneo)

Distant rumble (Thailand)

Which is the way
the right or the left?

William Blake

Sweet flower!
belike one day
to have
a place upon
thy poet's grave

William Wordsworth

Duchess (India)

Concentration (WA)

Caroline (Africa)

Let's play (USA)

Journey´s end (Lombok)

Slightly mad (Studio)